the Creative Writer's

Journal AND Handbook

Created by Trisha Sugarek

~~This spirited journal is designed to help writers open their hearts and minds. Much more than a journal for your creative writing, this handbook provides the writer with the 'how to's' of writing. Each blank, lined page has writing tips and quotes from other famous authors.~~

Notice

The Library of Congress has catalogued the soft cover edition of this book as follows: Sugarek, Trisha, The Writer's Journal/Trisha Sugarek - This is a journal/handbook. The suggestions and tips are solely the opinion of the author. The quotes were taken from various publications and the author takes no responsibility for the accuracy.

Made in the USA ISBN-13: 978-1499728750

Poetry and ink drawings by Trisha Sugarek
Cover and Layout Design by David White

To view all of the author's fiction and play scripts go to:

www.writeratplay.com

This journal belongs to:

_____

Table of Contents

Introduction

I created this journal/handbook to encourage other writers to pursue their dreams. It doesn't matter that you are just beginning your journey as a writer. Whatever your level of writing may be I have tried to create a book with a little something for everyone. Perhaps you have been journaling for years and want to try your hand at a story or poetry or a script. Or you are a more experienced writer and need a little inspiration to get you started on your next project. Regardless of your experience, I hope you find this book encouraging and a safe place to store your characters, your story outlines, and your private ideas for future stories.

Only when I began to write seriously did I come to realize that I had been writing my entire adult life. But back then I was just 'scribbling'. A thought I didn't want to forget, or a feeling I had to capture. Or a phrase that I was inspired by. Now that I am a published author and regular blogger people are interested in how I write, when I write, what inspires me, where do I find my stories. My story isn't that different from other authors I've had the pleasure to interview. I write because I have to. Most of my stories have found me so it's been easy to write them down.

"The difference between the right word and the nearly right word is the same as that between lightning and the lightning bug."

Mark Twain

How Do I Begin?

To stare at a blank page or screen….this is the scariest thing of all and sometimes causes a writer to give up before they have begun. Ray Bradbury said, "Writing is supposed to be difficult, agonizing, a dreadful exercise, a terrible occupation."

Forget for a moment about writing your great American novel or a world recognized poem or a Broadway hit. Begin with the first sentence. Don't let people tell you it starts with the first word…that's just silly. Practice writing that first sentence. For example:

'As I crossed the street I didn't see the bus bearing down on me.'

'I sat in the prison waiting room about to interview a convicted killer.'

"Slow down, Al," Vi screamed and laughed from the back seat. "You're gonna kill us."

'My first audition since I hit Hollywood and what if I fail?'

'The teacher grabbed my math work book and, marching to the front of the room, read my poetry aloud.'

'As the saloon doors creaked back and forth, the trail weary cowboys backed away when they saw him saunter in.'

"Mother must be spinning in her grave," Kitty muttered, as her chauffeur drove up the long driveway to the main entrance of the State Prison.

You have a story idea in your mind. Write the first sentence. Write two more that are different for the same story idea. Now choose the one that is your 'hook'. Ideally, the start of a book should capture the reader from the first sentence. This will launch your writing and your story.

Be certain that the main characters are well developed before you get too far into the story. There is a chapter here for character building and character analysis. Use this chapter to not only develop your fictional characters but to jot down your observations of real people that you see.

I can only tell you how my stories or poetry come to me. I'm certain it's different for everyone. An idea will pop into my mind. For several days it will germinate and then it starts to write itself. When my brain is full of ideas, dialogue, poem phrases, and people I have to sit down at my keyboard and transfer it. I frequently write 'out of order'. With fiction I will sometimes have the epilogue written months before the book is finished. I know I'm going to rewrite it anyway. A chapter might float along there on the page, unidentified, until I see where it naturally fits. The chapter is there in my mind and I know I'll use it, so I get it down lest I forget. And if, later, it doesn't fit, there's always the beloved delete key (a metaphor for your erasure or deleting what you've written in long hand.)

Do not feel as though you must have a whole poem or story ready to write. I'd never get anything written if I put that kind of pressure on myself. My hope is that you find this journal/handbook helpful in that way.

Now, write the first sentence of your first or newest story here:

"A will finds a way."

Orison Swett Marden

> "When I'm hungry, I eat. When I'm thirsty, I drink. When I feel like saying something, I say it."

Madonna

> **❝** For those who can
> do it and who keep
> their nerve, writing
> for a living still beats
> most real, grown-up
> jobs hands down. **❞**

Terence Blacker

TIP:

I rewrite and rewrite. I love my delete key. I let magic happen. I let my characters speak to me.

> "A woman must have money and a room of her own if she is to write fiction."
>
> *Virginia Woolf*

"People say I make strange choices, but they're not strange for me. My sickness is that I'm fascinated by human behavior, by what's underneath the surface, by the worlds inside people."

Johnny Depp

> **The road to success is always under construction.**
>
> *Lily Tomlin*

> "We relish news of our heroes, forgetting that we are extraordinary to somebody too."
>
> *Helen Hayes*

TIP:

When I'm not writing, I'm reading. I believe, as do many other successful writers, that reading other writers inspires me to be a better writer.

"To acquire the habit of reading is to construct for yourself a refuge from almost all the miseries of life."

W. Somerset Maugham

> **"Continuous effort
> - not strength
> or intelligence
> - is the key to
> unlocking our
> potential."**
>
> *Winston Churchill*

"I like to listen. I have learned a great deal from listening carefully. Most people never listen."

Ernest Hemingway

> "I'm in love with the potential of miracles. For me, the safest place is out on a limb."
>
> *Shirley MacLaine*

"You have to motivate yourself with challenges. That's how you know you're still alive."

Jerry Seinfeld

"We're all proud of making little mistakes. It gives us the feeling we don't make any big ones."

Andy Rooney

"Anything you put in a play -- any speech -- has got to do one of two things: either define character or push the action of the play along."

Edward Albee

Create Rich, Exciting Characters

This chapter is dedicated to developing the characters in your story. If you don't know your characters your readers will never get to know them or care about them.

After many years of writing, my characters show up in my head but it's my job to 'flesh them out'. Many times I will meet or see a character in real life and they inspire a character in my writing. But, it's still the writer's job to give them a story and breathe life into them.

If you're a new writer take the time to write it down here, using some of the tools listed. It's not the same as a few random thoughts about your character. Some intangible thing happens when you put pen to paper and get to know who your character is.

Picture the alphabet. Let's say that your character's appearance in your story (or in the script) is 'H' through 'M'. A good exercise that will lead you to a fully developed character is to write/create their story, 'A' through 'G'. This is their back story. Then write their story 'N' through 'Z'. (What happened to them after they leave your story.) Now you have created their entire life story. It will make your character so much interesting.

Another great exercise for the writer: Write down and describe their bedroom in great detail. What kind of bedroom would your character have? What color are the walls? What's on the bed? What's hanging on the walls? What part of the house/apt is your bedroom in? What's in the closet? Is your character neat or messy? Now read it back. It should tell you much about who your character is.

Read through your story and write down EVERYTHING the other characters say about the character you are creating.

These exercises do not have to show up in your book. They are merely ways to research and explore who your characters are.

When you are editing and rewriting be certain that part of your mind is looking for additional ways to flesh out your characters. Did you tell everything about them that your readers need to know about them? Did you tie up 'loose ends' of their story as your story progressed.

Explore your characters' motivations, goals, needs.

Villains versus Heroes: Heroes are easy to write. Your protagonist is honorable, friendly, good and kind. Villains not so much. There should be something that the reader can like about the antagonist. Perhaps it's a cutting wit. Maybe an act of kindness or something your reader can at least empathize with. Maybe it's something as simple as they are kind to their mother.

Using some of these tools try writing a character description/analysis here:

_____

_____

> **There are nights when the wolves are silent and only the moon howls.**
>
> *George Carlin*

_____

_____

_____

_____

_____

_____

_____

> **Intelligence without ambition is a bird without wings.**
>
> *Salvador Dali*

TIP:

Go to a local park, a ball game, a church, a bar, a grocery store, (you get the idea) and watch people.

> "Ninety-nine percent of the world's lovers are not with their first choice. That's what makes the jukebox play."
>
> *Willie Nelson*

"Between two evils,
I always pick the
one I never tried
before."

Mae West

> "Don't look forward to the day you stop suffering, because when it comes you'll know you're dead."

Tennessee Williams

"When I first started writing plays I couldn't write good dialogue because I didn't respect how black people talked. I thought that in order to make art out of their dialogue I had to change it, make it into something different. Once I learned to value and respect my characters, I could really hear them. I let them start talking."

August Wilson

> "Truth is like the sun. You can shut it out for a time, but it ain't goin' away."

Elvis Presley

"Love is the one emotion actors allow themselves to believe."

James Spader

> **If** you practice an art, be proud of it and make it proud of you. It may break your heart, but it will fill your heart before it breaks it; it will make you a person in your own right. **"**

Maxwell Anderson

> **"Anything you put in a play -- any speech -- has got to do one of two things: either define character or push the action of the play along."**
>
> *Edward Albee*

"I'm not funny. What I am is brave."

Lucille Ball

"Every secret of a writer's soul, every experience of his life, every quality of his mind is written large in his works."

Virginia Woolf

"When I played
drunks I had to
remain sober
because I didn't
know how to play
them when
I was drunk."

Richard Burton

> "Life is one grand, sweet song, so start the music."
>
> *Ronald Reagan*

> "The real reason for comedy is to hide the pain."

Wendy Wasserstein

“Hope is the feeling
that the feeling
you have isn't
permanent.”

Jean Kerr

**❝You can observe
a lot by just
watching.❞**

Yogi Berra

"If you took acting away from me, I'd stop breathing."

Ingrid Bergman

> **If you ask people what they've always wanted to do, most people haven't done it. That breaks my heart.**
>
> *Angelina Jolie*

> **It isn't what I do, but how I do it. It isn't what I say, but how I say it, and how I look when I do it and say it.**
>
> *Mae West*

> "Love yourself first and everything else falls into line. You really have to love yourself to get anything done in this world."

Lucille Ball

“Be yourself. The world worships the original.”

Ingrid Bergman

> **The most important thing in acting is honesty. If you can fake that, you've got it made.**
>
> *George Burns*

> "If you want to be successful, it's just this simple. Know what you are doing. Love what you are doing. And believe in what you are doing."

Will Rogers

> **If you do not tell the truth about yourself you cannot tell it about other people.**
>
> *Virginia Woolf*

> "The run I was on made Sinatra, Flynn, Jagger, Richards, all of them look like droopy-eyed armless children."
>
> *Charlie Sheen*

"The whole difference between construction and creation is exactly this: that a thing constructed can only be loved after it is constructed; but a thing created is loved before it exists."

Charles Dickens

"I am able to play monsters well. I understand monsters. I understand madmen."

Sir Anthony Hopkins

"Cock your hat -
angles are attitudes."

Frank Sinatra

> "You can design and create, and build the most wonderful place in the world. But it takes people to make the dream a reality."

Walt Disney

"You are never so alone as when you are ill on stage. The most nightmarish feeling in the world is suddenly to feel like throwing up in front of four thousand people."

Judy Garland

"Well, Art is Art, isn't it? Still, on the other hand, water is water. And east is east and west is west and if you take cranberries and stew them like applesauce they taste much more like prunes than rhubarb does. Now you tell me what you know."

Groucho Marx

"As kids we're not taught how to deal with success; we're taught how to deal with failure. If at first you don't succeed, try, try again. If at first you succeed, then what?"

Charlie Sheen

"Some of my best leading men have been dogs and horses."

Elizabeth Taylor

TIP:

Take from real life whenever you can. The most fascinating characters are real people.

> "I don't go by the rule book... I lead from the heart, not the head."

Princess Diana

"Don't let yesterday use up too much of today."

Will Rogers

> Some people see things that are and ask, Why? Some people dream of things that never were and ask, Why not? Some people have to go to work and don't have time for all that.

George Carlin

"Fiction is like
a spider's web,
attached ever so
slightly perhaps,
but still attached
to life at all four
corners. Often
the attachment
is scarcely
perceptible."

Virginia Woolf

"I had no desire to be an film actress, to always play somebody else, to be always beautiful with somebody constantly straightening out your every eyelash. It was always a big bother to me."

Marlene Dietrich

> **The way to get started is to quit talking and begin doing.**
>
> *Walt Disney*

> "I honestly think it is better to be a failure at something you love than to be a success at something you hate."

George Burns

"The writer must believe that what he is doing is the most important thing in the world. And he must hold to this illusion even when he knows it is not true."

John Steinbeck

Writing is an exploration. You start from nothing and learn as you go.
E. L. Doctorow

Storytelling

'Practice makes perfect.' Nothing could be truer when it comes to writing. Writing every day is essential to mastering your writing skills. It is the only trick, the only secret to becoming a writer and remaining a writer. Set a time when you are able to write for ten, fifteen, twenty minutes every day. Don't concern yourself with 'is it interesting, clever or even correct?' Just write! Your journal writing will keep you connected to your creative writing and your interior life. It promotes generating new writing. After a decade of writing plays, the thought of writing 300+ pages of a novel terrified me. I hope you will find, as happened to me, that your characters will help you write the story. Never let the enormity of the number of pages, doubting friends, well meaning family, or your own insecurity stop you from writing. Start with a short story and see how it goes.

You can write about anything. It is my hope that in this journal you will create rather than complain. The following section will provide you with private pages for your short stories, the beginning of a novel, your poetry or even a play script. Remember, I have included a chapter just for writers who would like to try their hand at stage play writing.

Balance your descriptive writing and your dialogue evenly. You might lose your readers if you describe each blade of grass. Your dialogue should be clean and sharp but remember to write like people really speak.

> **The profession of book writing makes horse racing seem like a solid, stable business.**
>
> *John Steinbeck*

"Planning to write
is not writing.
Outlining a book
is not writing.
Researching is not
writing. Talking
to people about
what you're doing
is not writing.
None of that is
writing. Writing is
writing."

E.L. Doctorow

TIP:

My journaling led me to healing, inspiration and the art of creative writing. I started writing down an idea which then became a stage play, then poetry, then books for kids. Then fiction. Write something every day.

> "A bookstore is one of the only pieces of evidence we have that people are still thinking."

Jerry Seinfeld

> **"This world is but a canvas to our imagination."**
>
> *Henry Thoreau*

"And by the way, everything in life is writable about if you have the outgoing guts to do it, and the imagination to improvise. The worst enemy to creativity is self-doubt."

Sylvia Plath

"There's nothing to writing. All you do is sit down at a typewriter and bleed."

Ernest Hemingway

> "When you are completely absorbed or caught up in something, (writing) you become oblivious to things around you, or to the passage of time. It is this absorption in what you are doing that frees your unconscious and releases your creative imagination."

Rollo May

"Invent yourself
and then reinvent
yourself, don't swim
in the same slough.
invent yourself
and then reinvent
yourself and stay
out of the clutches
of mediocrity.
Reinvigorate
yourself and accept
what is, but only on
the terms that you
have invented and
reinvented."

Charles Bukowski

> **"**Creative activity could be described as a type of learning process where teacher and pupil are located in the same individual.**"**

Arthur Koestler

"And in real life endings aren't always neat, whether they're happy endings, or whether they're sad endings."

Stephen King

"The reader, the book lover, must meet his own needs without paying too much attention to what his neighbors say those needs should be."

Teddy Roosevelt

Rewrite, Rewrite, Rewrite, Rewrite and then rewrite some more. Learn to love your delete key. Not everything you write will be worthy of keeping.

> "The stupid believe that to be truthful is easy; only the artist, the great artist, knows how difficult it is."
>
> *Willa Cather*

> **We are what we repeatedly do. Excellence, then, is not an act, but a habit.**
>
> *Aristotle*

> "There's a drive in me that won't allow me to do certain things that are easy."

Johnny Depp

> "Sometimes I feel like a figment of my own imagination."
>
> *Lily Tomlin*

TIP:

Be certain that your grammar and spelling are impeccable. Nothing distracts a reader, an editor or a theatre (that might consider your work) more than glaring spelling and grammatical errors.

"Art is not a
handicraft, it is the
transmission of
feeling the artist
has experienced."

Leo Tolstoy

“Imagination grows by exercise, and contrary to common belief, is more powerful in the mature than in the young.”

W. Somerset Maugham

> **The person who says it cannot be done should not interrupt the person doing it.**
>
> *Chinese Proverb*

> **Try again. Fail again. Fail better.**
>
> *Samuel Beckett*

> "I learned never to empty the well of my writing, but always to stop when there was still something there in the deep part of the well, and let it refill at night from the springs that fed it."
>
> *Ernest Hemingway*

"The aim of art is to represent not the outward appearance of things, but their inward significance."

Aristotle

> **The person, be it gentleman or lady, who has not pleasure in a good novel, must be intolerably stupid.**
>
> *Jane Austen*

"If I read a book and it makes my whole body so cold no fire can ever warm me, I know that is poetry.

Emily Dickinson

> "Ideas are like rabbits. You get a couple and learn how to handle them, and pretty soon you have a dozen."
>
> *John Steinbeck*

TIP:

If you're a new writer, begin by writing a story about someone or something that you know.

> "All writers are vain, selfish, and lazy, and at the very bottom of their motives there lies a mystery. Writing a book is a horrible, exhausting struggle, like a long bout of some painful illness."
>
> *George Orwell*

"Nothing you write, if you hope to be any good, will ever come out as you first hoped."

Lillian Hellman

"Be who you are and say what you feel, because those who mind don't matter, and those who matter don't mind."

Dr. Seuss

> **Good novels are not written, they are rewritten. Great novels are diamonds mined from layered rewrites.**
>
> *Andre Jute*

"Love. Fall in love and stay in love. Write only what you love, and love what you write. The key word is love. You have to get up in the morning and write something you love, something to live for."

Ray Bradbury

"Always be a first-rate version of yourself, instead of a second-rate version of somebody else."

Louis L'Amour

> "My role in society, or any artist's or poet's role, is to try and express what we all feel. Not to tell people how to feel. Not as a preacher, not as a leader, but as a reflection of us all."
>
> *John Lennon*

> **"If history were taught in the form of stories, it would never be forgotten."**
>
> *Rudyard Kipling*

"Oh! Do not attack me with your watch. A watch is always too fast or too slow. I cannot be dictated to by a watch."

Jane Austen

> "When asked, 'How do you write?' I invariably answer, 'one word at a time.'"
>
> *Stephen King*

> **Writing is supposed to be difficult, agonizing, a dreadful exercise, a terrible occupation.**
>
> *Ray Bradbury*

"I love writing. I love the swirl and swing of words as they tangle with human emotion."

James Michener

> "Continuous effort - not strength or intelligence-is the key to unlocking our potential.

Liane Cardes

"What is life but a series of inspired follies? The difficulty is to find them to do."

George Bernard Shaw

> "Every action we take, everything we do, is either a victory or defeat in the struggle to become what we want to be."

Anne Bronte

"There is a crack in everything, that's how the light gets in.

Leonard Cohen

"I wish I could write as mysterious as a cat."

Edgar Allan Poe

"When writing a novel a writer should create living people; people not characters. A character is a caricature."

Ernest Hemingway

> "The place where you made your stand never mattered. Only that you were there... and still on your feet."
>
> *Stephen King*

> **If** I give my characters free will, if I don't plot out the story and instead present them with a problem and watch them deal with it, they begin to take on a life of their own, frequently surprising me with the choices they make.

Dean Koontz

"Get your facts first,
then you can distort
them as you please."

Mark Twain

"The theater is so endlessly fascinating because it's so accidental. It's so much like life."

Arthur Miller

How to write a Stage Play

FOURTEEN TIPS TO GET YOU STARTED

1. **Format is very important.** Buy a play script or go on line to check out the approved format. When you submit your new play and it is not formatted correctly, they will not read it. There is software out there that offers auto-format. Below is a sample of the format. Notice character names are in CAPS and bold, followed with a period. Blocking (action) is in italics and always lower case if appearing in the 'line' of the actor. The character's name is bold and all CAPS in the blocking so that the actor is alerted that they has an action or a movement. A 'beat' is a dramatic pause or to enhance the pace of the speech. There is a space between dialogue and blocking but no spaces between the lines of dialogue.

Act One
Scene One

(***At Rise:*** *A loft studio in Greenwich Village. Late afternoon. While there are many paintings it is apparent that one subject has been painted again and again. Large windows overlook the street.*)

(**MONTY** *is painting at* **HIS** *easel.* **HE** *is a little paint smeared.* **HE** *hears voices from the street.*)

VOICE *(Off.)* Hey, beautiful! You're home early.

> *(Brush in one hand, palette in the other,* **MONTY** *crosses to the windows and   peers into the street below. The lilting laughter of a young woman is heard.)*

SAMANTHA. (Voice Off.) *(joking)* Hey, Mr. Murray. Your wife know you're trying to pick up women in the street?

VOICE *(Off.)* No…..and don't you tell on me. My old woman would give me what for…. bothering a young lady like you.

SAMANTHA. (Voice Off.) Your secret is safe with me…for a price.

VOICE *(Off.)* *(teasing)* Oh yeah, what's that?

SAMANTHA. (Voice Off.) Some fresh bagels from your bakery.

VOICE *(Off.)* You got a deal…I'll bring them home with me tomorrow.

SAMANTHA. (Voice Off.) Thanks, Mr. Murray! I'll look forward to them. Bye, now.

2. **Each page represents approximately one minute of time on stage**, depending upon blocking. So if you have a play that is 200 pages long, that won't work. Audiences aren't going to sit for more than one and a half hours unless you are providing a circus, a fire drill, AND an earthquake. Audiences are even reluctant to sit through "THE ICEMAN COMETH" a great classic by Eugene O'Neill. It runs close to 3 hours. You should keep your full length script to about 100 pages which equals 1.6 hours of stage time. For a one act divide that by 2. For a ten minute play your script should be from 10-15 pages.

3. **Leave lots of white space.** One day when your play is being produced, actors will need a place to make notes in the script during rehearsal. This is a sample of an actor'sworking script.   An actor usually 'highlights' their lines and writes the director's blocking in the margins.

4.   **The blocking** (in italics) is

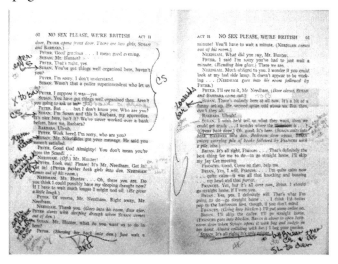

where you give the actors instructions on when and where to move. But, keep it short and sweet. Remember there will be a director who has their own ideas of where they want their actors to be. Be aware of costume changes in your writing. An actor can't exit stage left and enter stage right, seconds later, if you haven't written in the time it will take them to accomplish a costume change.

5. **Your script has to work on A STAGE.** If your story takes place in more than one locale, you have to be aware of the logistics of a 'set' change. So keep it simple to start. If you are ambitious in your set ideas buy a book on set design to research if your set is feasible. There are some wonderful 'envelope' sets that unfold when you need to change the scene. But you have to consider the budget; would a theatre have the money to build it? Always a worry.

6. **Dialogue: Now here's the hard part: everything you want the audience to know about the story and the characters, is conveyed in the dialogue.** Unlike a short story or a novel, where you can write as much description as you'd like, a play script has none of that. NO description. For example: If it's important for the audience to know that the character is a single working parent the dialogue must weave this into the story. Another character, talking about the single parent, can be used to tell the audience this fact.

7. **Cast:** Always, always tell the reader/director/actor **how many people are in the cast, their gender and ages.** In the beginning of your script you will have a 'character list' or Cast of Characters, stating the character's name, how they are germane to the story, and their age and physical appearance.

8. If you write a script with six to eight to ten men in it, **YOU ARE DOOMED**. Men are extremely hard to cast (they're just not out there and if they are, their jobs and families prevent them from auditioning) and so most directors are looking for a play with a reasonably small cast with more women than men. Under six to eight actors and two-thirds, women.

9. **Subject:** If this is your first play writing attempt, **write about something you know.** Maybe a family story. One of my first plays was about my days in Hollywood as an actor.

10. **Your dialogue is EVERYTHING.** You will be judged on **IT** alone. So try to be original, snappy, and funny. Even the most dramatic, tragic play has pathos. Be certain there are

NO typo's and check your grammar. Keep asking yourself, **'Can I write it better??'**

11. **The format for a stage play is entirely different from a screenplay.** Don't confuse the two. With a stage play, you are limited to what can physically be accomplished on a stage. With a screenplay you can have several locations, interior and exterior....pretty much whatever the budget will allow.

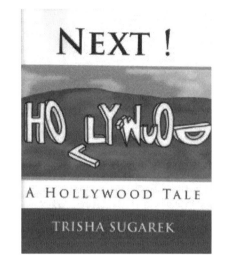

12. **Story Arc:** The end of the first act is the top of the story arch; keep your audience guessing during intermission so that they will not be tempted to leave during the break. Make them want to come back in to see how it all ends. Generally, the first act is longer than the second act.

13. **Terminology:** Be certain that you are well versed in theatre terminology. Stage left, stage right, down stage, blocking, beat/s, cross, enter, exit.

14. After you've written and rewritten your script, get some actors together and hold a reading, to hear how your play 'sounds'. This will help you immensely with your re-writes. Invite an audience and get their feedback.

Send your finished script out...then send it out again and.....again. Most community theatres are receptive to receiving scripts. Don't get discouraged! You WILL get rejected. I wish you could see my 'rejection letter' file! KEEP SENDING IT OUT!!

> "Language is wine
> upon the lips."
>
> *Virginia Woolf*

> **"Know from whence you came. If you know whence you came, there are absolutely no limitations to where you can go."**
>
> *Tennessee Williams*

"Acting is a nice childish profession - pretending you're someone else and, at the same time, selling yourself."

Katherine Hepburn

> **An actor is something less than a man, while an actress is something more than a woman.**
>
> *Richard Burton*

"What is not started today is never finished tomorrow."

Johann Wolfgang von Goethe

> **"I** can take any
> amount of
> criticism as long
> as I can consider it
> unqualified praise.**"**
>
> *Noel Coward*

"With any part you play, there is a certain amount of yourself in it. There has to be, otherwise it's just not acting. It's lying."

Johnny Depp

"If you string together a set of speeches expressive of character, and well finished in point and diction and thought, you will not produce the essential tragic effect nearly so well as with a play which, however deficient in these respects, yet has a plot and artistically constructed incidents."

Aristotle

"I think that as a playwright, if I detail that environment, then I'm taking away something from them [designers]. I'm taking away their creativity and their ability to have input themselves, not just to follow what the playwright has written. So I do a minimum set description and let the designers create within that."

August Wilson

"I hold more and more surely to the conviction that the use of masks will be discovered eventually to be the freest solution of the modern dramatist's problem as to how -- with the greatest possible dramatic clarity and economy of means -- he can express those profound hidden conflicts of the mind which the probings of psychology continue to disclose to us."

Eugene O'Neill

"I can't expose a human weakness on the stage unless I know it through having it myself."

Tennessee Williams

"I don't much care for large bodies of people collected together. Everyone knows that audiences vary enormously; it's a mistake to care too much about them. The thing one should be concerned with is whether the performance has expressed what one set out to express in writing the play. It sometimes does."

Harold Pinter

"The Welsh people have a talent for acting that one does not find in the English. The English lack heart."

Sir Anthony Hopkins

"The script is the coloring book that you're given, and your job is to figure out how to color it in. And also when and where to color outside the lines."

James Spader

"If you must have motivation, think of your paycheck on Friday."

Noel Coward

> **I may climb perhaps to no great heights, but I will climb alone.**
>
> *Cyrano De-Bergerac*

> "The apple cannot be stuck back on the Tree of Knowledge; once we begin to see, we are doomed and challenged to seek the strength to see more, not less."

Arthur Miller

> **Dreams are illustrations... from the book your soul is writing about you.**
>
> *Marsha Norman*

> "When I was a boy, I always saw myself as a hero in comic books and in movies. I grew up believing this dream."

Elvis Presley

> "I'm a writer. The more I act, the more resistance I have to it. If you accept work in a movie, you accept to be entrapped for a certain part of time, but you know you're getting out. I'm also earning enough to keep my horses, buying some time to write."
>
> *Sam Shepard*

> "There is just one life for each of us: our own."
>
> *Euripedes*

> "The term 'serious actor' is kind of an oxymoron, isn't it? Like 'Republican party' or 'airplane food."
>
> *Johnny Depp*

In the theatre, people talk. Talk, talk until the cows come home about journeys of discovery and about what Hazlitt thought of a line of Shakespeare. I can't stand it.

Sir Anthony Hopkins

"The subject of drama is The Lie. At the end of the drama THE TRUTH -- which has been overlooked, disregarded, scorned, and denied -- prevails. And that is how we know the Drama is done."

David Mamet

«Do you know what a playwright is? A playwright is someone who lets his guts hang out on the stage.»

Edward Albee

"The last collaborator is your audience ... when the audience comes in, it changes the temperature of what you've written. Things that seem to work well -- work in a sense of carry the story forward and be integral to the piece -- suddenly become a little less relevant or a little less functional or a little overlong or a little overweight or a little whatever. And so you start reshaping from an audience."

Stephen Sondheim

> **In** a play, from the beginning, you have to realize that you're preparing something which is going into the hands of other people, unknown at the time you're writing it.

T. S. Eliot

"One usually dislikes a play while writing it, but afterward it grows on one. Let others judge and make decisions."

Anton Chekhov

"New dramatic writing has banished conversational dialogue from the stage as a relic of dramaturgy based on conflict and exchange: any story, intrigue or plot that is too neatly tied up is suspect."

Patrice Pavis

"In playwriting, you've got to be able to write dialogue. And if you write enough of it and let it flow enough, you'll probably come across something that will give you a key as to structure. I think the process of writing a play is working back and forth between the moment and the whole."

David Mamet

> **❝** I get fed up with all this nonsense of ringing people up and lighting cigarettes and answering the doorbell that passes for action in so many modern plays. **❞**
>
> *Graham Greene*

"What shouldn't you do if you're a young playwright? Don't bore the audience! I mean, even if you have to resort to totally arbitrary killing on stage, or pointless gunfire, at least it'll catch their attention and keep them awake. Just keep the thing going any way you can."

Tennessee Williams

“I think that's foolishness on the part of the playwright to write about himself. People don't know anything about themselves.”

Edward Albee

" To me, the
greatest pleasure
of writing is not
what it's about,
but the inner
music that words
make. "

Truman Capote

> **"**Acting is a great way to make a living, especially when I consider what my alternatives were and probably still are...**"**
>
> *James Spader*

> **Get into the scene late, get out of the scene early.**
>
> *David Mamet*

"The art of the dramatist is very like the art of the architect. A plot has to be built up just as a house is built-- story after story; and no edifice has any chance of standing unless it has a broad foundation and a solid frame."

Brander Matthews

"I restore myself when I'm alone."

Marilyn Monroe

> "Writing has ... been to me like a bath from which I have risen feeling cleaner, healthier, and freer."

Henrik Ibsen

"A poet is a bird of unearthly excellence, who escapes from his celestial realm arrives in this world warbling. If we do not cherish him, he spreads his wings and flies back into his home-land."

Edward Albee

Poetry

Poetry is created in much the same way as other genres of writing. Something will trigger my poetic side. It might be a crushed carnation on an asphalt parking lot or the combination of smells from the biting snow air and a bonfire. The call of a wild bird or a memory from childhood. I begin with the first line of the poem. Perhaps I won't write the second line for several days. I can't stress this enough; it's okay if that happens.

Nothing else in the writer's world is more from their soul than poetry. Yes, there is structure that should be adhered to (Haiku) (Sestina) but the creation of words should originate from the soul. Flowing like life's blood from the heart.

In this section I have included other types/forms of poetry and their disciplines. What is the difference between a sonnet and an epigram? A canzone and a narrative? Every poet is attracted to different styles. Why don't you try one?

ABC: A poem that has five lines and creates a mood, picture, or feeling. Lines 1 through 4 are made up of words, phrases or clauses while the first word of each line is in alphabetical order. Line 5 is one sentence long and begins with any letter.

Ballad: A poem that tells a story similar to a folk tale or legend which often has a repeated refrain.

Ballade: Poetry which has three stanzas of seven, eight or ten lines and a shorter final stanza of four or five. All stanzas end with the same one line refrain.

Blank verse: A poem written in unrhymed iambic pentameter and is often unobtrusive. The iambic pentameter form often resembles the rhythms of speech.

Burlesque: Poetry that treats a serious subject as humor.

Canzone: Medieval Italian lyric style poetry with five or six stanzas and a shorter ending stanza.

Carpe diem: Latin expression that means 'seize the day.' Carpe diem poems have a theme of living for today.

Cinquain: Poetry with five lines. Line 1 has one word (the title). Line 2 has two words that describe the title. Line 3 has three words that tell the action. Line 4 has four words that express the feeling, and line 5 has one word which recalls the title.

Couplet: This type of poem is two lines which may be rhymed or unrhymed.

Dramatic monologue: A type of poem which is spoken to a listener.

Elegy: A sad and thoughtful poem about the death of an individual.

Epigram: A very short, ironic and witty poem usually written as a brief couplet or quatrain.

Haiku: A Japanese poem composed of three unrhymed lines of five, seven, and five morae, with three sets. Usually containing a season word.

Horatian ode: Short lyric poem written in two or four-line stanzas, each with its the same metrical pattern, often addressed to a friend and deal with friendship, love and the practice of poetry. It is named after its creator, Horace.

Idyll: Poetry that either depicts a peaceful, idealized country scene or a long poem telling a story about heroes of a bye gone age.

Lay: A long narrative poem, especially one that was sung by medieval minstrels.

Limerick: A short sometimes vulgar, humorous poem consisting of five anapestic lines. Lines 1, 2, and 5 have seven to ten syllables, rhyme and have the same verbal rhythm. The 3rd and 4th lines have five to seven syllables, rhyme and have the same rhythm.

Narrative: A poem that tells a story.

Ode: A lengthy lyric poem typically of a serious or meditative nature and having an elevated style and formal stanza structure.

Pastoral: A poem that depicts rural life in a peaceful, romanticized way.

Quatrain: A stanza or poem consisting of four lines. Lines 2 and 4 must rhyme while having a similar number of syllables.

Rhyme: A rhyming poem has the repetition of the same or similar sounds of two or more words, often at the end of the line.

Rondeau: A lyrical poem of French origin having 10 or 13 lines with two rhymes and with the opening phrase repeated twice as the refrain.

Senryu: A short Japanese style poem, similar to haiku in structure that treats human beings rather than nature: Often in a humorous or satiric way.

Sestina: A poem consisting of six six-line stanzas and a three-line envoy. The end words of the first stanza are repeated in varied order as end words in the other stanzas and also recur in the envoy.

Shakespearean: A 14-line sonnet consisting of three quatrains of abab cdcd efef followed by a couplet, gg. Shakespearean sonnets generally use iambic pentameter.

Sonnet: A lyric poem that consists of 14 lines which usually have one or more conventional rhyme schemes.

Tanka: A Japanese poem of five lines, the first and third composed of five syllables and the other seven.

Terza Rima: A type of poetry consisting of 10 or 11 syllable lines arranged in three-line tercets.

Verse: A single metrical line of poetry.

> "Poetry is just the
> evidence of life. If
> your life is burning
> well, poetry is just
> the ash."
>
> *Leonard Cohen*

> **Dare to be honest and fear no labor.**
>
> *Robert Burns*

"Two roads diverged in a wood and I - I took the one less travelled by, And that has made all the difference."

Robert Frost

> There's not a good poet I know who has not at the beck and call of his memory a vast quantity of poetry that composes his mental library.

Anthony Hecht

"An ignorance of means may minister to greatness, but an ignorance of aims make it impossible to be great at all."

Elizabeth Barrett Browning

"The heart of another is a dark forest, always, no matter how close it has been to one's own.

Willa Cather

TIP:

The great thing about 'free verse' is you can write your feelings, thoughts, without much structure. The more you write, the more you will feel the rhythm and flow. 'Free verse' is described as: It is an open form of poetry. It does not use consistent meter patterns, rhyme, or any other musical pattern. It thus tends to follow the rhythm of natural speech.

Beauty is not caused. It is.

Emily Dickinson

> "After the separation of death one can eventually swallow back one's grief, but the separation of the living is an endless, unappeasable anxiety."

Tu Fu

> "I'd rather learn from one bird how to sing than to teach ten thousand stars how not to dance."

E.E. Cummings

"And the first rude sketch that the world had seen was joy to his mighty heart, till the Devil whispered behind the leaves 'It's pretty, but is it Art?'"

Rudyard Kipling

"Doubt is a pain
too lonely to know
that faith is his
twin brother."

Khalil Gibran

> **No verse is free for the man who wants to do a good job.**
>
> *T.S. Eliot*

> **"...because to make a thing true all you've got to do is believe."**
>
> *Charles Bukowski*

"Poetry is the
rhythmical creation
of beauty in words."

Edgar Allen Poe

> "Poetry is the opening and closing of a door, leaving those who look through to guess about what is seen during the moment."
>
> *Carl Sandberg*

> "Blessed are the weird people–poets, misfits, writers, mystics...painters & troubadours–for they teach us to see the world through different eyes."

Jacob Nordby

> **As long as I retain my feeling and my passion for Nature, I can partly soften or subdue my other passions and resist or endure those of others.**
>
> *Lord Byron*

"The condition every art requires is, not so much freedom from restriction, as freedom from adulteration and from the intrusion of foreign matter."

Willa Cather

> "I took a deep breath and listened to the old bray of my heart. I am. I am. I am."

Sylvia Plath

> "To have great poets there must be great audiences too."
>
> *Walt Whitman*

> "The poet cannot invent new words every time, of course. He uses the words of the tribe. But the handling of the word, the accent, a new articulation, renew them."
>
> *Eugene Ionesco*

"Poetry is an echo,
asking a shadow
to dance."

Carl Sandberg

> "I'd rather be a could-be if I cannot be an are; because a could-be is a maybe who is reaching for a star. I'd rather be a has-been than a might-have-been, by far; for a might have-been has never been, but a has was once an are."

Milton Berle

"I am my own experiment. I am my own work of art."

Madonna

> "Poetry is when an emotion has found its thought and the thought has found words."
>
> *Robert Frost*

The soul should always stand ajar, ready to welcome the ecstatic experience.

Emily Dickinson

"Haiku poets ought to regard all aspects of creation as sacred and important, for each entity has an influence that, if we are openly aware, can be received by us, and which can give us deeper insight into the creation of which we are part."

Robert Spiess

Haiku Poetry

Haiku Poetry, **an ancient form of writing poetry from Japan**, is very strict in its discipline. Three sections of three lines each. The first and third lines, in each section, must be five syllables. The second line must be seven syllables. A reference to nature is usually found somewhere in the poem. The Sumi-E ink and brushwork you see here is also an ancient Japanese technique.

When I begin write Haiku, I don't worry so much about the structure on the first draft. I get my thoughts down and then start editing words (syllables) until I have the correct structure of 5-7-5. This works best for me and gives me more freedom.

Don't let the discipline hinder you… contrarily, let it free you. And the more you write in this time-honored style the more free you will be as a poet.

Miyamoto Musashi, a 15th century Japanese swordsman and ronin (the term for what we now know as Samurai) became renowned through stories of his excellent swordsmanship in numerous battles, even from a very young age. He was the founder of the Nitenryū style of swordsmanship and the author of The Book of Five Rings, a book on strategy, tactics, and philosophy that is still studied today. Miyamoto Musashi is widely considered one of the greatest warriors of all time. The samurai were expected to explore their artistic and philosophical side and most were known, not only for their prowess on the battlefield, but for their beautiful poetry.

By two masters….Yukio Mishima and Miyamoto Musashi. (Note: translated, the poetry does not keep to the exact discipline. Japanese poets used 'sound units' rather than syllables.)

The sheaths of swords rattle
As after years of endurance
Brave men set out
To tread upon the first frost of the year
A small night storm blows
Saying 'falling is the essence of a flower'
Preceding those who hesitate
—Yukio Mishima

A crow has settled
on a bare branch
Autumn evening
On a withered branch,
A crow has stopped
Autumn's eve
A lone crow
sits on a dead branch
this autumn eve

~~ Miyamoto Musashi

In Japan the Samurai/poets would frequently write Haiku before battle. Death poems were considered a necessity, graceful, natural, and emotionally neutral, in accordance with the teachings of Buddha.

Like a rotten log
half buried in the ground
my life, which has not flowered,
comes to this sad end.

Minamoto Yorimasa 1104-1180

I wrote the first draft of this poem in my car after leaving the UPS store. Was the entire poem suddenly there? Certainly not. But the first two lines certainly were. So keep your journal close at hand.

Forgotten Flower, forgotten love (Haiku)

Crushed petal, crushed stem

Flattened flower, Trampled love

Dead and dry flower

Crushed love, crushed heart, still

Packed down against the pavement

Crushed flower, crushed stem

Forgotten love, lost

Dried between sun and pavement

pages in a book

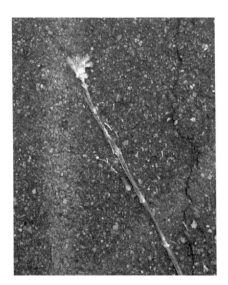

Samurai Song

    delicate blossom

    rests in the still gnarled hand

    bruised petals weep tears

    weary eyes open

    tiny cuts, the body bleeds

    peace still years away

    sun rise breaks the hill

    heralds another battle

    draw your sword and charge

               ~~Trisha Sugarek

Wind Horse

running free, wild, brave

tail streaming high in the wind

hoof pounding the earth

horses turn their haunch

to show their scorn for the storm

and nature's tantrum

allows man to think

he can command elegance

and tame the wild heart

~~Trisha Sugarek

The Seasons of the Sun

angle of fall's sun

so different from spring's rays

dapples the sun porch

end of hot summer

the crisp, sharp tang of fall's breath

smokes the air about

a waiting for sleep

under the blanket of snow

until spring sun beams

~~Trisha Sugarek

April's air stirs in
Willow-leaves...a butterfly
Floats and balances
                    ~~Matsuo Basho

Arise from sleep, old cat,
And with great yawns and stretchings...
Amble out for love
                    ~~Kobayashi Issa

An old silent pond
A frog jumps into the pond,
splash! Silence again
Autumn moonlight—
a worm digs silently
into the chestnut

Lightning flash
what I thought were faces
are plumes of pampas grass.
          ~~ Basho Matsuo (1600s)

> Do not seek to follow in the footsteps of the wise. Seek what they sought.

Matsuo Basho

"If you do not change direction, you may end up where you are heading.

Lao Tzu

> *One joy dispels a hundred cares.*
>
> Unknown

"When composing a verse let there not be a hair's breath separating your mind from what you write; composition of a poem must be done in an instant, like a woodcutter felling a huge tree or a swordsman leaping at a dangerous enemy."

Matsuo Basho

"Haiku is not a
shriek, a howl, a
sigh, or a yawn;
rather, it is the deep
breath of life."

Santoka Taneda

> **Do not seek to follow in the footsteps of the wise. Seek what they sought.**
>
> *Bashō*

"In haiku the half is greater than the whole: the haiku's achievement is in what it omits."

Robert Spiess

> **Every moment of life is a Haiku.**
>
> *Unknown*

"Dare to love yourself
as if you were a
rainbow with gold
at both ends."

Aberjhani

"Real haiku is the soul of poetry. Anything that is not actually present in one's heart is not haiku. The moon glows, flowers bloom, insects cry, water flows. Go beyond the restrictions of your era, forget about purpose or meaning, separate yourself from historical limitations—there you will find the essence of true art, religion, and science."

Santoka Taneda

"Calligraphy of geese
against the sky-
the moon seals it."

Yosa Buson

"Rejoice at your life for the time is more advanced than you would think."

Japanese Proverb

> "Freedom from desire leads to inward peace."

Lao-Tse

> **"The greatest revelation is stillness."**
>
> *Lao-Tse*

"For these few days the hills are bright
with cherry blossom.
Longer, and we should not
prize them so."

Yamabe No Akahito

Also by
TRISHA SUGAREK

<u>Fiction</u>
"Women Outside the Walls"
"Wild Violets"
"Song of the Yukon"

<u>Series * The World of Murder</u>
"The Art of Murder"
"The Dance of Murder"
"The Act of Murder"
"The Angel of Murder"
"The Taste of Murder"

<u>Plays</u>
"Ten Minutes to Curtain, Vol. II" A Collection of short plays

For the young Actor:
"Cook County Justice"
"Scent of Magnolia"
"The Guyer Girls"
"Emma and the Lost Unicorn"
"Stanley the Stalwart Dragon"
"The Exciting Exploits of an Effervescent Elf"
"Women Outside the Walls"
"NEXT! A Hollywood Tale"
"Sins of the Mother"
"Possession is Nine Tenths"

<u>Juvenile Fiction</u>
"Stanley the Stalwart Dragon"
"The Exciting Exploits of an Effervescent Elf"
"Bertie, the Bookworm and the Bully Boys"
"Emma and the Lost Unicorn"

<u>Poetry</u>
"Butterflies and Bullets"
"The World of Haiku" with Sumi-E Artwork
"Haiku Journal" -- a companion book
"Moths and Machetes"

To learn more about the author and her books, visit
www.writeratplay.com

Made in the USA
Middletown, DE
19 December 2018